Speakers

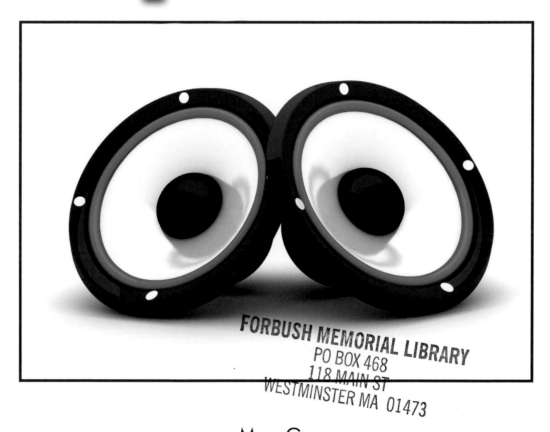

Meg Greve

rourkeeducationalmedia.com

Scan for Related Titles
and Teacher Resources

Teaching Focus:
Concepts of Print- Have students find capital letters and punctuation in a sentence. Ask students to explain the purpose for using them in a sentence.

Before Reading:

Building Academic Vocabulary and Background Knowledge

Before reading a book, it is important to set the stage for your child or students by using pre-reading strategies. This will help them develop their vocabulary, increase their reading comprehension, and make connections across the curriculum.

1. *Read the title and look at the cover. Let's make predictions about what this book will be about.*
2. *Take a picture walk by talking about the pictures/photographs in the book. Implant the vocabulary as you take the picture walk. Be sure to talk about the text features such as headings, Table of Contents, glossary, bolded words, captions, charts/ diagrams, or Index.*
3. Have students read the first page of text with you then have students read the remaining text.
4. *Strategy Talk – use to assist students while reading.*
    - *Get your mouth ready*
    - *Look at the picture*
    - *Think…does it make sense*
    - *Think…does it look right*
    - *Think…does it sound right*
    - *Chunk it – by looking for a part you know*
5. *Read it again.*
6. *After reading the book complete the activities below.*

Content Area Vocabulary
Use glossary words in a sentence.

amplify
cone
current
electromagnet
vibrates
volume

After Reading:

Comprehension and Extension Activity

After reading the book, work on the following questions with your child or students in order to check their level of reading comprehension and content mastery.

1. *What are the main parts of a speaker? (Summarize)*
2. *What is the purpose of the cone inside the speaker? (Asking questions)*
3. *In what ways do you use speakers? (Text to self connection)*
4. *What does amplify mean? (Summarize)*

Extension Activity

Think about all the ways you use speakers in your life. How do they enhance your life? Now think about other places that use speakers. What would happen if there weren't any speakers at sporting events or concerts? How would we hear a presidential candidate give a speech? Create a table and identify the pros and cons of speakers.

Table of Contents

Turn It Up!

Speakers can be smaller than a dime, or as big as a truck. Their job is very simple. When you turn on your radio, iPod, or television, speakers deliver the sound your device makes.

How Do Speakers Work?

Do you like to listen to music or listen to books on CDs? When you press play, the player turns the sound into an electric **current**.

Inside the speakers many parts work together to produce sound.

Speakers have two kinds of magnets. One magnet cannot move. The other magnet is an **electromagnet**.

magnet

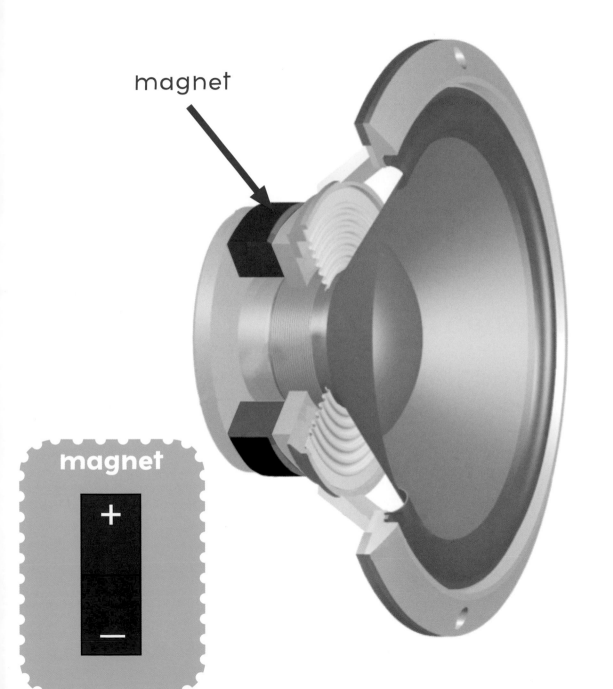

magnet

+

−

The electromagnet is a wire coil that **vibrates** when the electric current passes through it.

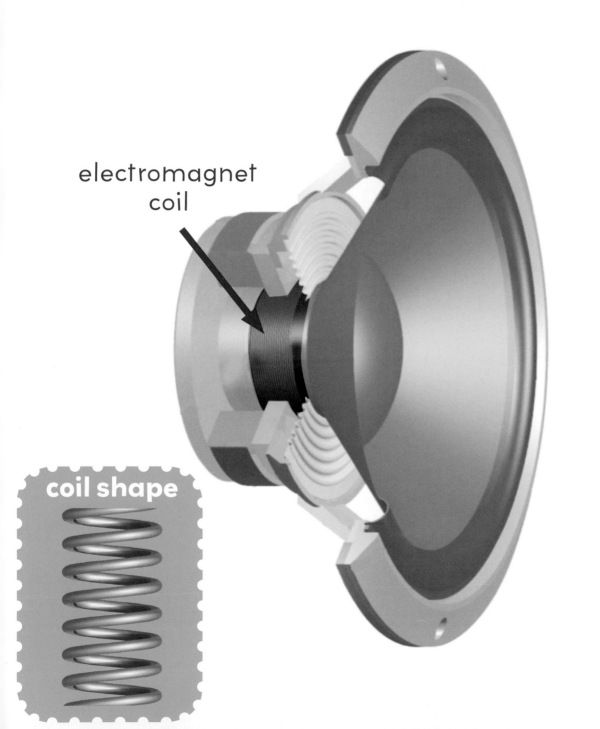

electromagnet coil

coil shape

13

The coil is attached to a cone. The cone moves. It vibrates back and forth. The **cone** makes the sound louder, sending the sound out into the air.

You may not be able to see sound waves, but if they are loud enough, you can feel the vibrations in the floor, walls, or on the speaker.

cone

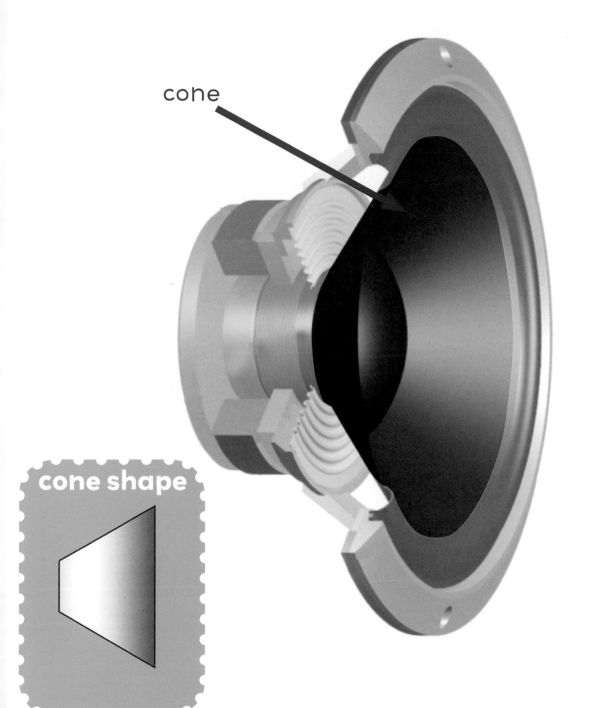

cone shape

Loud or Soft?

Speakers **amplify** sound, making it louder. You can change the speaker's **volume** by turning it up or down.

If your speakers are too loud, you can damage your ears and even lose your hearing.

Speakers allow us to listen to music, movies, books, and even the sound of a lion's roar. Whatever device you are using would not be as much fun without speakers!

Try This!

Make Your MP3 Louder

1. Find a medium-sized metal or glass bowl.

2. Turn the volume on your MP3 to the highest level.

3. Put your MP3 player in the bowl. It will be even louder.

The shape of the bowl is like the cone on a speaker. It amplifies the sound!

Photo Glossary

amplify (AM-pli-fye): To make something louder.

cone (KOHN): An object with a round base and a pointy top.

current (KUR-uhnt): The movement of electricity through a wire.

 **electromagnet** (i-lek-troh-MAG-nit): A magnet that forms when electricity moves through a wire coil.

 **vibrates** (VYE-brayts): To quickly move back and forth.

 **volume** (VAHL-yoom): How loud something is.

Index

Websites to Visit

www.stevespanglerscience.com/lab/experiments/category/light-and-sound
www.brainpop.com/science/energy/sound/
www.sciencekids.co.nz/sound.html

Meet The Author!
www.meetREMauthors.com

About the Author

Meg Greve lives in Chicago with her husband Tom, and her two children, Madison and William. When she is in the car by herself, she turns up the volume on the radio and sings along!

www.rourkeeducationalmedia.com

PHOTO CREDITS: Cover © zevemski; title page, 18 © vladru; page 4 © jarp; page 5, 22 © Avesun, design56, Peresanz; page 7, 22 © Vietrow Dmytro; page 8 © sashahattam; page 9 © kutberk; page 11, 13, 15, 22, 23 © Svjo; page 16 © Jon Larson; page 17 © Nicole Young; page 19 © ktaylovg; page 20 © flashgun, hanibaram; page 21, 22 © Jani Bryson

Edited by: Jill Sherman

Cover and Interior design by: Jen Thomas

Library of Congress PCN Data

Speakers / Meg Greve
(How It Works)
ISBN (hard cover)(alk. paper) 978-1-62717-644-6
ISBN (soft cover) 978-1-62717-766-5
ISBN (e-Book) 978-1-62717-886-0
Library of Congress Control Number: 2014934236

Printed in the United States of America, North Mankato, Minnesota

Also Available as:
ROURKE'S
e-Books